SOME WORLDS FOR DR. VOGT

MATVEI YANKELEVICH

SOME WORLDS

FOR DR. VOGT

 BLACK SQUARE EDITIONS
NEW YORK CITY
MMXV

COVER IMAGE: *Barcroft Branches,*
2014, by Hannah Whitaker
Courtesy of M+B Gallery

DESIGN: Shari DeGraw

ISBN: 978-0-9860050-7-7

BSE BOOKS ARE
DISTRIBUTED BY SPD:
Small Press Distribution
1341 Seventh Street
Berkeley, California 94710

800-869-7553
orders@spdbooks.org
www.spdbooks.org

An independent subsidiary
of Off The Park Press

TO CONTACT THE PRESS,
PLEASE WRITE:
Black Square Editions
1200 Broadway, Suite 3C
New York, New York 10001

CONTRIBUTIONS TO BSE
CAN BE MADE TO:
Off The Park Press
972 Sunset Ridge
Bridgewater, New Jersey 08807

(please specify your donation
is for Black Square Editions)

SOME WORLDS FOR DR. VOGT

Each form is a world.

KAZIMIR MALEVICH,
"From Cubism and Futurism to Suprematism"

1

Eucalyptus leaves stir, a slow
tremble outside the automobile
factory. There is
a world, an image
undisturbed
by speech. The article
missing from *the gates.*
VW crossing the plaid field.
You could say *of vision*
but you don't. There
is a world, a repetition
undisturbed
by rhyme. The soccer player
breaks his ankle thanks
to the game he loves:
small sacrifice. Poor trees—
knowing so little
of their tragedy: to sway
to shake in the wind, to
sough and bow.

11

On what field of vision
does the horse graze
on fallen pine needles? Where
is the man welding green
light by the glowing
pink cross on the corner?
There, in a world, a relation
unknown, unhindered
by the vast potential
of introspection. Truck
full of cane. A truck-full
of laborers. Factory road:
sugar on this side, beer
on the other. Graffiti.
Farms. Fires by the culvert
keep down the brush. Hawk
crests a telephone wire — circle
culture. White egret jutting
out of the marsh where cattle
leave little to the earth. Is it bone
below the bark?

III

As sight cools into sound, or digs
into sound? Dog cools off
in the lagoon. *Andante* digging
in the *piano.* There's a world.
And if you had seen it
at the beginning
you'd have seen it
begin. If you had seen it begin
you would know how it felt
to be nothing becoming
something, but now
you are everything
becoming nothing
to speak of, a limit
bearing down, approaching
zero, as a towel dries, as a tire
degrades; as a coinage dissolves
first into cliché, then idiom,
ceasing to be the thing and leaving
only meaning to swallow it
as time swallows the rocks, or
moves them. A world:
in the revolutionary moment,
in a hammock, a gilded ballroom,
in the hollow of a violin hidden
under the lid of a piano. Do you
need to say *black,* say *shiny*
say *grand?* The image: no more
labor for the mind. The piano
you fail to note is broken. Imagine
the dust. If you want
add spiders.

IV

In this intimate conversion
of telling you: a world. The gate
drawn with a curtain,
the column rebuilt, the jail
reconstructed to be
locked again. *Where did you
go wrong?* At the same time
the plastic bottle feels
in your hand the same
as the wind feels in the branches
of the spindly pine, or the rain
in the fronds of the palm. Delta
waters in the mangrove
roots. The bite of an insect,
the bite of distilled spirits —
compare these things. There
is a world in the comparison
between souls, an argument
amidst trees (to name them:
botany, or worse).
The threads of the screw
last only so long. Bolts
and hinges also come loose. Here
in the bloom, the hummingbird
prevails, the golden bee hovers,
the air bears down on the canopy
as furniture music.

v

A wall of glass: almost accurate
as a leaf follows the sun — its veins
an argument against the bark
or the word for its escape
from it. In a net, in a country —
in the fray. To counter vision
the draughtsman moves his elbow
along a line. Type falls into place
by way of pneumatic tubes. And
far away, behind the page, there is
a world: an administrative error,
a disjunction no longer visible
on the horizon, in serifed grasses
or reeds of a swamp. The chair
in the sand never upright. Somewhere
between serpent and eagle there is
a world, or a relativity; it
hangs there, humming
a tune like St James Infirmary,
St Louis Blues, or "When
the sun goes down…"

VI

The wind cools you, but why
the coffee lukewarm? Long waves
of ignorance wash over your toes.
The swimmer leans into the current,
dries in the wind. Between is a world
of shadow the alphabet follows — the rule
of the letter. Smell the copper
dust under the graver, the scent
of black, wove paper, and nitric acid
in the rough basement. Take it
to a mirror, or let this mirror come
to touch everything that exists in order
to be crammed into a book, even metaphysics,
even hips. See how it's bound
at one edge, suggesting entrance, or
what is said is done. What's left
of this world is color, the flapping pulp —
transparent white. The turning
of a page: a minute, a new year. When
the fishermen throw their nets there is
a very quiet applause and sometimes a giggle
hardly auditory, like the gap between two
insect landings on the map of the empire.

An absolute scale of resemblance and disresemblance
establishes measures that are music in the actual world.

ROBERT DUNCAN, "The Structure of Rhyme"

VII

A as in apophasis. An ant moves along.
It is going somewhere with blind faith
in green promise. It meets whatever
it meets on the way. Determination
takes the place of destination, traversing
every needle of a fallen pine. The ant's
unsettled mind paces with six legs
eschewing stasis. Followed by your pen
its path is traced but makes the ant
turn in ways unknown to its instinct
so that the ant is getting away from itself.
The plane it traces shoots out a space
whose dimensions are at once auto-telic
and implausible in this world. To do
something else, fill the general up
with data as moments against time.

VIII

And if the comfortable ladies sit
sprung like lionesses in the sun,
toes curled in silver sounds of
Slavic cell phone usage, low-toned
pricey and pre-possessed, not
to say worked-over, then that's
a world of life, if only vacated.
And if rhythm falls where it might
it is the window between here and
the next connection that sheds
considered light upon its beating—
a step unstitched from stepping
i.e. gerund cancelled. Yet, say you
another direction looks downward
in the fall and where this rhythm
goes one cannot follow. No small
work is this against big words.

IX

To take your mind off the defibrillator,
the operating table. The umbrella takes
a rain check, leaving the sewing machine
to its workaday hum. Permeable living:
shadows on wet cement. The surf
or just the highway sounding
over the tree line. A chair in a room
against a wall. Apartment complexes across.
A way to say what isn't said: Eros—a world unto
itself. *It's not all clockwork,* this isn't a Texas
tenor in Watts, nor a circular book, it turns out
after all: one of many chosen few.

X

To disconnect this from that takes some gumption,
but what about keeping on? The thing that fell behind
the dresser could be found someday, sooner or later—
back there is a world in the future, a bad line of poetry.
Take this wrist. Keep it. It only serves one connection
now lost on you. *It's like a notebook.* "It's been
a long night," *you feel it.* These gestures are letters
no one thinks anymore to map. Here's to the gap
between what we planned to accomplish and the
thing in front of us. Raise your glass: this is
the thing itself, what's left after we drink to it.

XI

The pen brings your arm
closer to the pad as on the page
a letter sidles up to its neighbor.
In proximity there is a type of duration
interpreted as sound, which in itself
consists of nearer proximities: a world
dedicated to musicians. A repeating
moment or recurrent dream
of stepping into a flux where you become
stationary, vertical, bisecting the lines
of motion — new rock in old water.
Home or wasted country? Heron on a hill
descending to the stream, moss on the stones.
Your beer cap glows in the momentum.

XII

A lush taxonomy breathes deep in the blue wood.
Mowers, harvesters along the perimeter. A park
or no place, which is the same. A crack
in the pavement from one side of the road to the other
in the shape of lightning. Steel, light with holes, lifts
a rectangular sign above human heads, slanted
in relation to the two yellow lines touching this
world to that. Numbers and arrows and letters —
twigs of wood. Splotches of grass amid dirt
and pebbles. Squat iron hydrant, its
flattened spouts. Water running free beyond it
in the shadow of dark limbs — things that stay
uncarryable away, the unmistakable
preciousness of a theory of artifice.

The complete world
Is likeness in every corner

LAURA (RIDING) JACKSON, "World's End"

XIII

The wave comes frame by frame
in a medieval repetition, like a sound
repeating the thing but coming before it
as a name. The glow of what is about to
occur and the blur of it passing the lens
too quickly. This, the parabola of wet sand
against a dry beach. A few grains of salt
on your lapel and collar. A familiar voice
from over one shoulder. A stray hair
repeating the sand's curve, but stuck
to stubble. Shells abandoned by pioneering
shellfish move into a physics of metaphor —
a tautology sets sail
under the breeze of air conditioning.

XIV

The pleasure of certainty and the pain
of the same certainty — performing
the grimace in a mirror image.
The beauty of a breast in your hand
and the reflection of table-settings
in bedroom behaviors. Why not hold
the body all day? There is a world —
an ideal one — in the instant of
the holding, or sudden gaze into nothing.
Also a world in the patter of rain, otherwise
known as a defense of poetry, a genitive
shadow in the preposition, the process
by which nail enters wood or needle
entertains fabric. This material
world: tooth pressing on tooth
to grow the vine.

XV

Swish swish and a couple of noodles
to make a landscape. A kind of broken bench,
the bended armrest, a trace of plush or
velvet in green iron. A man in long shorts
building a door jamb, but no walls around,
the door open. Lowered gates. Rattling fences.
Gray in gravel around green — the observation
of observation. Correspondence of color
or conversation of light? To make things
white again, blink the eyes.

XVI

The path of a snake on water — a line
natural to the word. With time
the line wrests itself from the branch,
from lightning, from the path of the bug
coming for the corpse. The bug in your
starched shirt: a phantom
touching a nerve. A world in a flash
of contours, but without shape.
The contour of a wave or of wind
but not its path — a shape you can
somehow signify in a straight line.
The margin tightens: a pain
grows dull. The swimmer wades
into the water.

XVII

That's what all this means of thought
here or there, in this point of not
starting at all. *Hold on,* you whisper.
What's to hold on to? Was there
before holding tired of this world
a sum of parts, or parts of a whole?
How time's hand does to skin, to bark,
to flesh of statues shading summer talk.
Aged urns and vases of perception;
sharp furs and tatters of sensation:
O, failure of the five to grasp the depth
in crumbling curb and garden step.

Enter the world,
a species already sufficiently inured to tragedy

ANNA MOSCHOVAKIS, "The Tragedy of Waste"

XVIII

A new world springs up where the old world
nearly leaves off. The pawpaws are cut back
to reveal a field of maize, a comfort of crows'
grainy call, tongues that click. Paddles
beat the heavy ribs of arched sculls. At
a yellow crossroad you decide to make
a left and what happens after is history or
just a job to hiss and spit at. A racket
or a lever, a level and a rule. Sweat stains
the page of oriented labor, no longer
disappearing in the dirt of tilled rows.

XIX

The comfort of an arm, a screen,
a calendar, a folding chair. A moon
fit for a king, a level of comfort
driven down by rising
barrel prices. To say *there is*
no hope for us but in meaning
and nonetheless, somehow
what replaces a banal pub
on the corner is more
generic even. Everywhere
things getting it right. You
walk by, smell the motivation.

XX

A boat. A moving sale.
A party undisturbed
by invitations. A mislaid
vocab. Price tags in the wind.
Surveyor bending to the scope.
Yellow reeds looking to forms
of potential thought. A cool
breeze through a competitive
model. The point of a dagger
missing, cut off by a framing
device made between wood
and linen. You could say
outside, or keep quiet.

XXI

In the conversion, a world comes to light
but not the world, actually. Or so you
might think. Or actually, in order that
you might think it. In order that that
world be perceived it must convert.
Or else who knows what the fuck is it?
Some kind of universe we're up against?
Worse: You take it on your own terms
even when you say you're taking it on
its own terms. In the lovely world over
there are some unfamiliar terms. Maybe
they're in your stomach, a world you can't
identify with even as it turns inside you.

XXII

That world flows through — rather
in that world everything flows together:
a common world. The chimney in disuse.
The smokestack — bricks and vines:
an image of industry as natural, inevitable,
primary. When it comes to
allegiances told through the hues
and heraldry of robes of boiled silk
no matter how... they speak
of fall foliage. Shrub oaks take
a vow the color of rust. Crickets
beat the earth outside — their typing
sings of lower desires, that pieces
should remain pieces
until the picture of a world emerges
of its own accord from music.

The term.   The fore-world.
Gone from care.

EDMOND JABÈS, "Well Water"

XXIII

There is a world different from any
other that is happening, now, occurring
in order to push this world into the past.

XXIV

     ... the cadaver climbs
toward other astronomies, beyond
the bed and the bath. Like blood
from a rock — wine, Jura, distant mind.

     ... a call for papers
in White Plains. Serifs advertise
fast food at the rest stop. Hands
over the mouths as over the lens.

     ... the changes play
to skipping — a record of failure
to meet the world. An infinite refrain
falls over the writing hand.

XXV

Pose a world as a tautology, or an equilibrium —
a state of balance, or static. Something like
the river flows — already redundant. What
in fact is its shape? For instance, someone
gave you this beer so you can't do anything
about it. You can drink it as long as you stand
relatively still, describing to yourself the view
or the way the tree trunks lay in the northern
woods, leafless then, save for the ground cover,
so that vision is not a noun, but the un-
achievable form of the verb *reading.*
Legere: Greeks choose to speak; Romans
pick through the ruins. All this is well known
but bears repeating. Cherry blossoms in the rain:
the season's emotional efficacy. To chew the crust,
another way to bite down. Even
the shapes of Eros, you know, are finite.

XXVI

Readymade as in ready to wear. Nails
like mushrooms with their floppy caps
or chinese hats. The body — cracked flesh
of synthetic putties and adhesives. Where's
the cookie tin? The linoleum? Chosen origin
of what world? Cast legs and torso down
the stairs, more than once, shard to
diamonds, or givens, for instance: A gray
mustache, almost fifty and still remembers
something, tugs hoodie down, pulls up
his denim, packs cigarettes hard against
a white palm. An ant, particular
variety, scurries over pitted
marble. A girl in clean black coat
in crisis over the absence of a Starbucks. What
is this world? Who are these people?

XXVII

Is this what you are seeing in this world?
Stand up for a little shade, or the comfort
of something known to few: a crooked chair
or bent-up bench, with dead leaves here
and there from last season, a bourgeois pleasure
in craft away from the assembly line of
experience. A cobble-stoned alley in cherry
blossoms, the consequence of *petit* desire:
paté in a bar. And a physical memory of that
other spring, its affair, a whole autobiography
in wisdom teeth. Waddling over the hill, spring
a light jacket. Sensation of almost abandon
the to-dos. You worked hard to get where
you are being the only one on the porch
where the patio furniture needs painting in
an endearing, lonely sense — here begins
the recuperation of your time, as if a
mnemonic device would suffice to recapture
the water of melting ice.

XXVIII

Trees leaf while mountains shimmer.
An architecture of bumpy triangulation
pulling their weight up to a taper. Outside
the phrasing there is a world that may
never come. A farce of bounded visions:
imperial nostalgia. A rhythm or a slide through
a wheel. All the insides spilling forth and
outside the furniture has taken to the streets,
set up makeshift shop to counter
the movement of numbers, to couch
the specter of concepts. To be
outside the period, awaiting what won't
come, as if at a wake backward, watching
the horizon for the event, or vice-versa.
The ground literally swells, heaves like
ocean, breathes like air, forgetting
its previous location as one forgets one's
phone number, one's own face. Worlds
begin with oblivion.

And I'm the world.
But the world's not me.

DANIIL KHARMS, "The Werld"

XXIX

Things are said to be out there
different from things that are
said unto being, or seen as
being there. And objects—
they float in inane rhythm
reversing the hammer and
the nail, undisturbed
by humanism, broken cartons
and folded-up individuals,
bathed in light. Some
thing can go wrong. You're
considering what it is and all
you have is a smile, a pine
desk, and parched papers
under the wine.

XXX

In the shape of a thing, another.
Fire in the match. Take out
the wood and leave it alone or
strike it. That is this, over there.
To bring it closer, almost
to the point of exception.
The thing maps a thought, all
mapping corrupted by the new
world. You make an idea of it.
Chart an object from life, cut
it out of it. And what's that left
in your hand?

XXXI

An image of the wind as vast,
vapid as the sea it sweeps
or the leaves swept up in it
as *animals in the alphabet*—
only what is so small stays
put. The dense world left
behind breathes its last
repetition, an illusion
of village life. The draft
might follow the original—
December 6th, or 7th?
In fact, ardor as
empty as *everything*
moving with the tides
or counting fingers.

XXXII

Not personal, this life
if you look out
over the tenements.
Original disappearing
act — a coming
that is not a going
for instance, in railway
tunnels, in
history, i.e., in what
happened before. Behind
the wheel, a rut, a
never finished thought.
Some thing to be
exact about, not easy
to say, or spit it out.
It's about to last
a long time
now, or
not at all.

XXXIII

Better to drink
the mouth itself
to avoid speech
that worlds exist,
books, some "k"
sound, with no
attachments, no
apps, yet to become
a speech triangle.
Better breathe or
close up shop, dream
of triumphant
peanut brittle. *Who's
to say?* — a way
to say better
off not knowing.

Outside

outside myself

there is a world,

WILLIAM CARLOS WILLIAMS, *Paterson*

XXXIV

                       ... so, posing a line
in repose, passing the time
instead of time passing, you
may contemplate some
meaningful coherence even
now fragmented into segments

as a shoulder jutting from
behind a garden urn on which
it leans, hair attached backwards
as spider legs, to make a fragment
of a head, a face turned away
never to be more than image

imagined in expectation, i.e.,
a contemplated form, the more
seductive thereby promise
of meaning; its beautiful
constructs, or *a way of putting it*
doesn't in the end matter — line

wrestles with words and means
in the glade or shade of cool
grotto until worn out where
it breaks at a point over the hills
with tradition, as the surveyor
folds the tripod of his scope

over a bee in the grasp
of an ant in the dirt, as *as* points
to a simultaneous resemblance,
unfilled, unconsummated, yet
reciprocal, all-consuming in
its decor—a drowsing line

in lieu of a revised totality in
sunlight's daytime sense, a
line, then, at leisure to
describe (as in *un-write*)
the shape of a day off—
a patter not for sake of art—

to celebrate a sabbath
that is useless to this world
of labor relations, useless to
you, too, now, following the line
with a working finger, that is
a finger that has been made

by time to represent your work,
entire occupation, nimble, severe,
its rings of skin, etched crosshatch,
half moon over a frayed
horizon tell of the wash
of waste. Outside

where nothing cuts, nothing
joins, someone is calling on
this phone as if a line tethers
to the world, whereas in fact
it circumscribes another: *It's
for you, Dr.*

199. "This in which," i.e., the world in its relations.

RON SILLIMAN, "The Chinese Notebook"

There was just the animal in the world

LESLIE SCALAPINO, "The eating and walking
at the same time is associated all right"

XXXV

The space between us is being
monitored by satellite to judge
the relative movements toward
and away, but the space stays
the same. The words *my face*
form on your lips as if mistaken.
In this identity — a world
of succor; no, wait, you've
been buffaloed

by many mirrors. Move
into the next available seat:
in plain sight, a world. Is this it?
Is this language language? No
form in speech? What's locked in
the furniture — also a body, but
at a significant remove. Let it be
a mild, coalescing body or body
politic, to sate your taste for the state.

XXXVI

Take this as is and make it a world.
In the translation there is a clearing,
in the clearing is a spring. Warmth
in the train. Bad news in a letter.
Look out at the stadium:
they howl and stop howling.

Ask them why is there orange light
or people who care only of honor
who won't step down? What principle
takes precedence over the sick at heart?
Let them sleep one last hour
before their throats close.

XXXVII

Animals cut into
parts, crawling, scurrying
along the soil. You pick
one up and gesture
us to look. In your hand
is an organism, you
are an organism. What
can come of this —

for instance, if your arm
is a prosthetic device?
Your beckoning: a sign
mechanically reproduced, also
a drawing in the air,
a calligraphy that reads
black on white, a tautology
packed in ice, a frozen repetition
of ancestral digits.

XXXVIII

Make it new, then
erase it. Or, make it new
then do it again. To put your arm
through your arm, hand through
hand up to the shoulder,
repeat with legs into
a letter, to make

a loudhailer of your head,
to hover uneasily
as a geometry above
abstract planes, wings
as a swimmer uncrossed
against the air, as crosses
of propellers spin to suns.

XXXIX

As you sit to watch this night fall
back straight to a stone wall,
as a rhythm of another past
shadows this present to surpass
its evening cypher and reveal —
as metals melded into steel
square a mirror — this face of glass,
unknown as owned by one that passed
this way before, but is the same

approximately, as a thing is named,
tightly wound as in wind smoke's
patient swirl, a circle in a lock,
similar to sound, as real
as goes water in a fickle wheel,
not to be breathed aloud, but heard —
one word paces in another word
as evening clouds' pink against black
swell from bank to blank bank.

THE OTHER WORLD

T E D G R E E N W A L D, bumper sticker

XL

Brick by brick, the factory is taken apart.
Some time ago the world was a terrible
place to be and it still is a place where
coffee is served hot or iced, that today
is no different and wine sleeps inside
a bottle *on a day just like today*. It wills
itself stirred from sleep. Then there's all
that was good in the past, including
the headlights of passing cars filtered
by hanging spruce. The rust of the world
and the world of rust. Things like bridges
and train tracks pushing words
around the past from town to town:
write to me, write me when you can,
write me as soon as you can. There
was the hope that chins wouldn't double
anytime soon. There was the world
as you knew it, same as known. The smell
of pencil shavings and pen caps, mushrooms
after summer rain, construction dust
slow to replace emptiness, cranes overhead.
There was the day before, and the day after,
roads in both directions, another coin
to flip between us. A dry breeze lifts the page
and lets it fall, doesn't come back.

XLI

Spaces get rarer but wider as day fills in.
The purpose of night: cutting dawn's ribbon,
kerning out. Farther out the pines grow shorter.
When do you begin to speak so that no one
can hear? The line — where is it drawn
between what is an idea and what is a thing?
The line is the sign for it, or a name. The glimpse or
the grasp take note of it without the proper distance
and all these questions — you can ask them at the edge
of the parking lot, standing along straight demarcations
of spots. Beyond the blacktop begin the sands,
the shrub, broken chunks of curbstone, leftovers
from the dig. A self-reliance in thick weeds
and in slick grass, a gumption. You imagine evading
taxes in a wood where there is a world of symbolic
meaning in the branches of the shaggy undergrowth.
These worlds, the points where branches meet
in the removal of depth-of-field, are — as the stars
map endpoints in a chart of lines — no more
than serifs snapped on tips of invisible letters. Meeting
in the eye, these intersections are after all only dots
of depth conspiring to drop dimensionality
or the memory of space, mocking transparency
as hats deride heads.

XLII

The difference between punishment
and repentance — a blue blade of crabgrass.
Some escape the war, others
tend the bodies, avoid their glances.
So many ways to go in this world
clouded by vision, narrowed to a crust of bread —
for example, in the hand of the child
an offering to the ghost at the door.
After so many years, call it recognition.
There is a world of ghosts, all those
who survive, as if life could go on mechanically,
as if there were any *outside*. You plant a tree
to replace the tree that died. The effort
matches the task, masks the nervous whim.
Late birds settle in its branches to pick out
the bugs encoding the bark. You have more
to say but no inroads. Turn this way, fire.
The other, ice — or maybe wind.

XLIII

There is a storage room to fill
for later on so as not to clutter
the present scenario. It could be
spoken of in language that is
yet to surface, a cavern scribble,
the writing of nature. Gold
teeth of forgotten ancestors
hide out in a shoe box with broken
earrings and a lock of hair tied
with a shoelace wrapped
in a silk scarf. Smoke
or the sound of it curling—
loss without recoup. Personal
pharmacies of struggle, tailored
suits of government issue
surplus. Conversations repurposed
into clotheslines resplendent
with beach towels. There are doors
too heavy to open, a world
of confident postponement.
Broken shale in the fire pit.
The full moon as seen on TV
through a dirty window.

The animation of f-stops — a receding image
of lines erased or laced up to almost tighter
than the shape held framed. In passing
an unwinding proves knotted. The ball
of the pen a point size smaller than
the ant's own head. A morning that lasts
a day, the beginning and end of May.
The naming of February, or drizzle —
the sound following the scent. The segment
at the back of the ant-as-time-line falls away
into the evening light above the wood
of a picnic table. The light over the a/c
removed from a side window: a world
that encompasses its own gaze. A sock
pulled up falls down again. The tug,
dissipated, folds in on itself, drawing
an area of doubt over tall foreheads.
This map of probabilities asks chance
to take the clouds for instance, or as
example. A day that could have been
a very divers day, buried with sharded
pots. Against will, a sky-blue path
to the woods: the world that's
taken you for a given.

XLV

Sometimes electricity itself makes noise —
buzzing without will or instinct. This world
also fades. The impulse — original, electric —
goes elsewhere or to a remove from a body
tired of itself. Nor can it be said to act at all
if a light goes out when the circuit is broken.
It buzzed in lightning bugs and the clouds
moved on. The clouds where the sun set
on that day were full of rosewater,
geranium-pink, then slowly turned
gray, soft, and blended with the pallor
of the atmosphere. You noted it
to be most still that afternoon to evening.
There were barbecues firing up
for summer, their cinders burned long.
The leaves were still but the ants bustled.
No rustle in the trees while the water
flowed and the sky surged slowly
in circles. You lift a hand and watch it stay
in place, and what is that burn from
from the other day, and what is it like
to be still while you still are in this world?
You can push the air around a while longer.
You can dress yourself and cast shadow.
Onward, Communists, the banner flaps
in the film. "Onward!" the soldiers sing.

ACKNOWLEDGMENTS

Parts of this book, in earlier versions, first appeared in *Aufgabe*, BOMB, *Brooklyn Rail*, ETZ, *Fell Swoop*, *Frieze*, MAKE *Magazine*, *Mandorla*, *Quill Puddle*, and *Sun's Skeleton*. Many thanks to the editors of these publications.

The first few sections served as text for the film *Some Worlds* (2012), made collaboratively with Jeanne Liotta, presented online at BOMB, first screened publicly at Counterpath Gallery, Denver, Colorado.

Extensive excerpts, with intermittent commentary, were published as "(The Making of) Some Worlds for Dr. Vogt" in Koo Jeong A's *Constellation Congress* (Dia/Yale, 2013).

"Dr. Vogt" was the title of an installation of drawings by Koo Jeong A at the Dan Flavin Art Institute, in Bridgehampton, New York, where the first draft of this work was performed on July 21, 2011. I am grateful to several people who at various times, as members of the Dia Art Foundation staff, supported the development of the poem: Yasmil Raymond, Jeanne Dreskin, Kelly Kivland, Michelle Piranio, and especially Christine Shan Shan Hou, and the Dan Flavin Art Institute's Grant Haffner. Thanks to Koo Jeong A, whose work provided a motivation and a title.

For conversations around and about this book during its composition, and for encouragement, I would like to thank Anselm Berrigan, Jen Bervin, David Daratony, Christina Davis, Richard Deming, Karen Emmerich, Nathaniel Farrell, Ben Friedlander, Ellie Ga, Peter Gizzi, Julia Goldberg,

Nora Griffin, Carla Harryman, John High, Kristen Kosmas, Nancy Kuhl, Ann Lauterbach, Andrea Libin, Jeanne Liotta, Brenda Lozano, Anna Moschovakis, Michael Newton, Daniel Owen, Jeremy Sigler, Mónica de la Torre, Patricia Treib, Chris and George Tysh, Barrett Watten, and John Yau.

Thanks to Gabriela Jauregui, who unwittingly brought me to the first glimmers of this poem, and to Hannah Bacon, Alan Gilbert, Anna Moschovakis, and George Tysh for precise and generative editorial advice. It is impossible to express enough gratitude to Nathaniel Farrell, who gave of his ears and eyes to countless revisions.

Lines from Edmond Jabès taken as an epigraph appear in a translation by Anthony Rudolph; epigraphs from Kazimir Malevich and Daniil Kharms appear in my own translation. A line from Tristan Tzara in a translation by Nick Moudry begins poem xxiv. In poem xxv, I translate (freely) some lines from a poem by Arkadii Dragomoshchenko.

This poem is dedicated to the memory of my grandmother, Elena Bonner (1923 – 2011).

Matvei Yankelevich is the author of a poetry collection, *Alpha Donut* (United Artists), a novel in fragments, *Boris by the Sea* (Octopus), and several chapbooks. He is the translator of *Today I Wrote Nothing: The Selected Writings of Daniil Kharms* (Overlook/Ardis) and co-translator of *An Invitation for Me to Think* by Alexander Vvedensky (NYRB Poets), which won the National Translation Award in 2014; his translations have appeared in many periodicals and several anthologies. Matvei is one of the founding editors of Ugly Duckling Presse, where among other things he curates the Eastern European Poets Series and co-edits *6x6*. He teaches variously as an itinerant lecturer with frequent engagements at Columbia University's School of the Arts, and is a member of the Writing Faculty at the Milton Avery Graduate School of the Arts at Bard College.

One thousand copies of *Some Worlds for Dr. Vogt* were printed and bound at Thomson-Shore in Dexter, Michigan. The poem is set in Eric Gill's Perpetua and Gill Sans types.